Bill M Burton

Edited by Debbie L Burton

As the sunlight
As the sunlight shines brightly on us
It will give us strength to really grow
The natural way of life is tremendous
Knowing we can create our portfolio

Bridges
All bridges that make you cross over
From hardship to your real destiny
Can be shared, so others can turn over
To a life of full belief and certainty

Our foundation
The water that sustain us with life
Is a universal gift for every being?
Doesn't hurt to think of the wildlife
Our lifeline we should be overseeing

Vital trees
The vital trees give oxygen for everyone
Whereas the rock is truly, our foundation

Copyright © 2018 by Bill M Burton

Burton, Bill M. 1959
Title: **Quotes of Vision – Decisive Initiatives**

Published by Burton Publishing

ISBN 978-1-989047-00-2

All rights reserved. No part of this publication may be reproduced or transmitted, in any form or by any means, without the prior written consent of the publisher.

Edited by Debbie L Burton

Cover designed by
digimaxcreative.com

Burton Publishing
111 St. Lucie Drive,
North York Ontario,
Canada, M9M 1T4

billburton@rogers.com

Preface

My main objective in life is to inspire those who are searching for a better way of living. These poems have a foundation of their own; they are intended to lift you up when almost everything seems to be going wrong. These poems were written from actual experiences and what I have observed from my surroundings. I would like to thank my teachers DeLou Maureen Powell and B.B Bent of the Junction Junior secondary school in St, Elizabeth Jamaica W.I for believing in me so many years ago, my sister and editor Debbie L Burton, my son Davey C Burton for his website and computer genius, Christopher Thomas, Micah Clarke, my family and friends. I would like to salute all the uplifting poets of today and those who have gone before me. It's truly difficult holding down a nine to five job and writing at the same time. To write with clearness and understanding our minds and heart must be rested. These poems are written for the like-minded who wish to try a freshness of doing instead of giving into the struggles of life. Poetry can give us strength to carry on when unwanted worries lingers. It brightens our life when we need that extra push in the right direction. (The key to everlasting happiness, is to give love freely to all human beings)

Bill Burton

Foreword

In this life we all have duties to carry out as survivors, responsibilities that have never been taught to us by any school or institution. I'm fully convinced that Bill is one out of many who have something of substance to deliver into this world, in a divine order that's coming from our creator. I've known Bill for the past year and during my acquaintance with him, I notice that at no time was he afraid to express his views and opinion for the oppress conditions of the oppressed. Most of his life he has personally experienced the condition which people of African descent have had to encounter. This has played a great role in our development. Bill has carefully examined the effect that these conditions have on our people which created such a dim future. He wants to change this way of life for the betterment of his people through his inspired messages. I believe this book will deliver a clear message that will draw us closer to examine and reassess our selves. Bill knows if this cycle of life that has been forced upon our people continues, it will destroy the human race.

Micah Clarke

DESTINY 1

- Get up 2
- Not too late 2
- Rebuild 2
- Only bridge 3
- Strength 3
- When it seems 4
- At the edge 4
- Designed 5
- Own destiny 5
- Be awaken 6
- Your guard 6
- Dead-end 7
- Much sweeter 7
- Insatiable 7
- Once too often 7
- Its toll 8
- Reclaim 9
- Essence of freedom 9

Spiteful dagger	9
True guidance	9
Dignity	10
No one	10
Into gear	10
This time	10
Curfew	11
Our goals	11
Desire	11
Fire within	12
To believe	12
Bills	13
The upbeat	13
Still wonder	14
A new avenue	15
The takers	15
Each time	16
Must depart	17
Our efforts	18
Face the test	19

Our energy 19

Got to be ready 20

Real answers 20

Isn't a race 21

Short cut 21

Our life 21

Recover 22

Own initiatives 23

Promises 23

A quiet voice 24

Kept alive 25

Retreating 25

New start 26

When doubt 27

Passionate living 27

New urge 28

Embrace 28

Go the distance 29

Short cuts 29

To richness 30

Only medication	30
Not too late	31
Working people	31
Lightless alley	31
Color or creed	32
Undertake	33
Out of the rough	34
Doers	35
Kept alive	35
The puzzle	36
Fertile seed	37
Abundance	38
New light	39
My view	40
Common sense	41
The lead	42
Smart work	42
In sync	42
Quest on time	43
Don't be discouraged	44

Will be yours 44

Turn up the torch 44

Come about 45

Right direction 45

No middle ground 46

Love our-self 46

Providence 46

A true virtue 47

To our rescue 47

Reach deeper 47

Clay-like dolls 48

NATURAL QUALITIES 49

Without them 50

Our appreciation 50

Way home 51

Joy everlasting 52

Ray of light 52

Alside 53

Mist and rain 54

Spur tree hill 54

Flat bridge 54

Bog-walk 54

Such beauty 54

Vibrant 55

My weariness 56

Summer time 57

Scented flowers 57

True light 58

Guide us 58

Safe flight 58

Meaty fruit 59

Always relish 60

So much warmth 60

Giant fruits 60

The river bank 61

Tried to focus 61

Cool breeze 61

Beautiful sight 61

From the air 62

Place to remember 62

A sea of birds 62

Warmth and grace 63

Mother Africa 63

The bread winner 64

Listen 65

Smiling faces 66

Magical ride 67

Sincerely 68

WORLD-WIDE EPIDEMIC 69

Vanity 70

Suffers 70

Quiet lunch 71

Our brood 72

When groom 72

To permeate 73

If you are different 73

All over the nation 73

Back of a hearse 73

Catastrophe 74

Undone 74

Terrified rage 75

Very cold 76

Permanent run 77

Whatever 77

Increase 77

Trust 78

Useless 78

Revoked..78

Deliberately 79

Ever do 80

Unwanted rage...............................80

KINDNESS & DEVOTION 81

Love knows no color 82

Why pretend 83

No need 84

Been replaced 84

Anymore 84

For a life time 85

Take my heart 85

A little bit closer 86

Pretentious 86

Lonesome 86

Got to dear to love 87

No boudaries 87

A splash of forget me not 88

Love or lust 88

So much energy 89

Our life 90

Keep at bay..90

Different 90

Move forward...................................90

Negative people................................90

Living free..90

Her beauty 91

Our African Queens 92

Hidden Mask 93

COLDNESS & LAZINESS.........95

Infected seeds 96

Intrigued 96

Covered 96

Guide ourselves 97

Kind of urge 97

Corrupted human 98

Overloaded fools 98

Elusive influence 98

Spoils 98

Hard to handle 99

The needy 99

Rainy day......................................100

Dwindling......................................100

Insomnia..101

Sometimes.....................................101

World's ego...................................101

Long road 102

Convoluted 102

The bait...102

Slender string	102
To enhance	103
Blisterd heart	103
Years of pain	103
Perish	103
Fare share	103
Appetite	103
Withered	104
Courage	104
Long overdue	104
Reinstate	105
Our Suffering	105
Can't escape	105
Distracted mind	106
Clashes	107
Selective	107
No longer pretend	107
Your lies	107
Conceited	108
Downsizing	109

Self-centeredness 110

Crying for peace 110

Disregarded 110

Lawmakers 111

Their feast 111

Designed 111

Hidden taxes 112

Morality 112

Drips slowly 113

For riches 113

Unbearable 114

One by one 115

Yours and mine 115

Won't cry 116

My luck 116

Bit of sanity 117

At the expense 117

Betrayal 117

Emptiness 117

Fruitless 118

XIX

Working class 119

Cubbyhole 119

Decayed 120

Global quest 120

Blood of others 120

Seekers 120

To refresh 121

New insights 121

It's time 121

Labeled 122

Pencil pushers 122

Nagative 123

Both ways 123

Self-respect 123

Will pass 124

Unexpected 124

PERSONAL QUOTES.................125

Reach on time................................126

Good benefits 126

I do believe 126

Excuses..126

Be loyal 127

Regardless 127

Missgiving.....................................127

Elusive...127

Birthdays 128

A mother.......................................128

True example................................129

Caring ways..................................129

Greatest trait.................................129

Never far.......................................129

Destination 130

Clear to see...................................130

Happy birthday.............................130

Looking pretty..............................131

Family tree....................................132

Great mom 132

Giving 132

Abundant 132

A natural trend 133

Together 133

Free 134

Time 134

Guiding hand 134

Everyday task 135

New beginnings 135

Calm sea 136

Life can 136

Persistency 136

Tranquility 136

Chief aim 137

Willingness 137

Enlighten 137

Desire 138

Ponient love 138

Each other 138

Kindness	139
Share	139
Respect	139
Goodbye	140
Will always	140
Kind hearted	141
Cherished	141
A rear gem	142
Assurance	142
True grace	142
What's right	143
Many storms	143
Forward	143
Way of life	144
True hearted	144
Inline	145
A doing heart	145
The ships	145
Won't be bleak	146

From the heart 146

Repatriate 147

Together 147

Cross over 148

Tolerance 148

Useless hate 148

Around us 149

Some days 149

My genuine rose 150

Guiding Light 150

Bright taste 150

Prim 150

Gentle prose 150

ENDLESS TIME..........................151

    Ups and downs 152

    Beyond 152

    Petite existence 152

    Late before 153

    Brown grip 153

    Calmness 153

    Three sisters 154

    Gaze quietly 154

    Gentleness 154

    Prosper 154

    Way of life 154

    Our love 155

    Good- bye 155

    God of mercy 155

    Our Sally forever 155

    Time will 156

    Cherish 156

    Flower of love 156

    Restraint 156

Flying high	157
Free of hate	157
Encouragement	157
Forever love	157
As we linger	158
With maturity	158
Calm and quietly	159
Forgiveness	159
He teaches	159
Dearest love	160
Giving agenda	160
At peace	160
Our teacher	161
So clearly	161
Trueness	161
A fisherman	162
Abundantly	162
Parted waves	162

Destiny

Get up
Don't wait too long to get going
It's time to do what we're doing
Whenever you receive the get up and go
Take action before the light turns to low

Not too late
Have sat down and let the world go by
Now our basic needs will be deny
It's not too late to stake our claim
Even though our will is almost drain

Rebuild
We'll have to work harder to rebuild
That doesn't mean dreams can't be fulfilled

Only bridge
Sharing is the only bridge for caring
And caring has a true base in sharing
Haven't we stumbled long enough?
Time to help each other out of the rough

Strength
Strength we can muster from our sorrow
As long as we pay attention to the horror
Leading by examples is most competent
It shows how we can be really proficient

When it seems
When distraction intensifies, keep your focus.
When it seems that all solution runs out, still
Keep your focus.

At the edge
When you're at the edge of
Giving up, that's when factual wisdom will
Explode.

Designed

If we are free, why do they constantly harm
Us? We'll try to find a job and before they're
Through glancing at our resumes, they'll tell
Us we're not really qualified. This system is
Designed to keep us down and now we'll
Have to break ourselves free.

Own destiny

We'll have to
Create our own destiny, cause that's the only
Cure for this disease. This stigma of we don't
Know what to do, must be expose from their
Dreadful "bluff"

Be awaken
Mental poison is the choice of weapon now-
a- days, if we take a short nap; we might be
Awaken by a mental smack.

Your guard
Whatever we are
About to undertake, be on your guard for
Persuading crooks.

Dead-end
Won't feel sorry when I leave this dead- end
Labor of grind, because my goal is waiting to
Be achieved.

Much sweeter
The air I breathe will be much
Sweeter, no longer surrounded by evilness;
Life will be more fulfilling.

Insatiable
Scrooges with faces of greed, saturate the
Entire place. I can see the blood they crave
Slowly dripping down their insatiable faces.

Once too often
My strength had stop to rest once too often,
And now awaken by man's self-indulgence; I
Must push on through before it causes more
Suffering.

Its toll

Clear to see we have enchained our mind,
Body and soul as this crushing work has
Taken its toll. To find our right place in life, a
Balance with true living we'll have to initiate.

Reclaim
We Africans are the only race, who's in a
Massive stagger. Because robbers had tried to
Destroy our history, we haven't the drive to
Reclaim our way of life.

Essence of freedom
Today everything is
Inactive; our whole life is nothing but a
Struggle. In order to reinforce the essence of
Freedom, we must begin to read again.

Spiteful dagger
Slavery has interrupted the human race,
Which pierce the heart like a spiteful dagger?
We got to escape from this hurtful game,
Then share the essential encouragement with
Our children.

True guidance
At this moment if we are too
Weak, true guidance we got to find. Shouldn't
Wait on chance to fix our problem, it's time
To steer our existence in the right direction.

Dignity
Today it's time to break free
From misguided suggestion
Time to reclaim our dignity
Finding a workable solution

No one
No one care for us but us
Careful of much falsehood
Pretending to be glamorous
Patrolling the neighborhood

Into gear
They have a pleasing trait
Waiting to shift into gear
Unworkable mental state
That will bring us despair

This time
Now I have gotten a real break
This time I'll make no mistake

Curfew
Keep the faith in what you do,
Or you will be put in a curfew.

Our goals
Time is really of the essence,
As our goals is in the presence.

Desire
You can accomplish your desire,
Remember you've got to perspire.

Fire within

To us, Garvey brought the fire within
Paving the road that means everything
Now we must keep the flames alive
In spite of how difficult it is to strive

To believe

Big boulders may stand in our way
But we can push them out the way
The only tool we need is to believe
It carries out action we'll conceive
Can feel goose bumps in my nerve
Knowing what my goals can serve

Bills
Bills we'll have to tackle
As our brain start to crackle
Remember you are not alone
Everyone's crush to the bone

The upbeat
Even though things are tight
Search not for an idle flight
Resist the murky downbeat
And persist with the upbeat

Still wonder

Yesterday I didn't have a clue
Today I don't know what to do
Years have come and gone
Still wonder what's going on
Taking myself off the fence
Now seeing the recompense

A new avenue
Our joints sound like they need lubricating,
And our pocket books all worn out.

The takers
There will always be the takers desire, at the expense of
Those who do the work. Let's find a new
Avenue, before our strength is totally wasted.

Each time

For us, time's truly running out,
Now we'll have to travel a new route.
Each time that we're making headway,
These illusive thoughts get in the way.
After we have studied and understand,
It's time to follow through with a plan.

Must depart

What is it that's holding me down?
In reality, I just can't move around.
What is it that's holding me back?
In my existence, I'm way off track.
Must depart from this merry-go-round,
Or my whole survival will run aground.

Our efforts
When receiving a sense of urge,
Our laziness must be purge.
As we build our fire stronger,
Our efforts will truly surrender.

Face the test
Some of us love being second best,
Truth is we don't want to face the test.
We all will start out oh so very strong,
Then lose sight of where we belong.

Our energy
The more we are around uselessness,
It directs our energy into total distress.
Slaying real devotions in what we do,
Before our aim in life can come true.

Got to be ready

Got to be ready to face everyday task,
Then in the sunshine you can bask.
Not wise been down over daily hinder,
Cause our sanity we shouldn't surrender.

Real answers

If we really want to escape this mayhem,
We can find the solution to our problem.
Real answers don't come in one session,
It takes many tries before it can function.

Isn't a race
Go at your own pace,
Cause life isn't a race.
Don't try to impress,
And get very careless.

Short cut
Tempted to take short cut,
You may end up in a rut.
Taken your own direction,
You'll get true satisfaction.

Our life
Our life will be complete,
If we can see beyond defeat.
We can take other direction,
With motivating satisfaction.

Recover

A feeling of giving up comes over me,
But now is the best time to really see.
Got to recover my obtainable vision,
That I've lost through my indecision.

Own initiatives
Taking orders from others we'll embrace it,
Being self-reliant we'll turn our backs on it.
We want to enjoy the fruit, but we're too lazy to
Instigate our own initiatives.

Promises
We'll trade our birthright, for any would be promises,
While the recipients flaunt their weight
Around. We can be the brains behind the
World trend, yet we don't want to transcend.

A quiet voice
Through the nature of life
Hardship will cut like a knife
We'll give our all
But still we'll fall
A quiet voice will speak
To guide us when we're weak
Keep your head up high
Then you must continue to try

Kept alive

My option had been disconnected,
It must be found and reconnected.
No matter how hard it is to strive,
My will to do, must be kept alive.

Retreating

Sometimes I've felt truly beaten,
But it's only a bit of retreating.
Tomorrow will bring a new day,
And my drive to strive must obey.

New start

Why waste time trying to be perfect, grab a
Hold of life, follow through, and then reflect.
Now that we've shared the compass of true
Inspiration, isn't it time you deal with the
Situation. Life's too short, for you to be
Completely smart, if only you will make a
Brand new start.

When doubt
Life is a challenge, taking the easy way out;
You should never indulge in. When doubt had
Sneak in from the back door, don't go easy on
The culprit, cause it's not your friend, it only
Want to wear you out.

Passionate living
In your quest for
Passionate living, storms of hindrance always
Close at hand. Don't give into this negative
Traitor, remember your dreams, and you'll
Succeed.

New urge
Monday and I'm back in here again,
With machines they don't maintain.
Tried to justify why I'm still here,
Knowing these bosses don't care.
However I'm sensing a new urge,
That my laziness should be purge.

Embrace
The time has come to leave this place,
Then plant a seed that I can embrace.

Go the distance

When we utilize persistence,
We'll surely go the distance.
It's so easy to walk away,
But go forth without delay.
Those who tried to cut you down,
In time will vanish underground

Short cuts

Short cuts will destroy your luck,
Then leave you permanently stuck.
Persist though your patience is thin,
Cause sitting down you will never win.
Victory for some will take a long time,
That doesn't mean their goal isn't in-line.

To richness
If we want to cross the road from poverty to
Richness, we must be determined. When it
Seems the whole world has turned its back on
You, you must be determined.

Only medication
When there is no other technique left to try,
We must still be determined. Determination is
The only medication, which we can use in any
Situation.

Not too late
Sometimes we're chained mentally to a
Factory, thinking it is satisfactory. But it's
Not too late, to leave that hurting place, even
If you have to do it in many a phase.

Working people
Survival is now getting worse, and
Dishonesty is in automatic speed. The need to
Want it all is soaring, as the life of the less
Fortunate gets deploring. No one listens to the
Cry of the working people, because they are
Controlled by well- paid lawyers.

Lightless alley
Sadly we are chained mentally, to a never-
Ending lightless alley. Isn't it time we take a
Glance and see how deep we're sinking? How
Much tougher can life get? It's time to
Acquire a bona fide action
Without apology.

Color or creed

As these poems flow from my heart,
They are designed to give us a new start.
Whatever gender, race, color or creed,
We should help whoever is in need.
Embracing selfishness is not unique,
Let greed stumble with its technique.

Undertake

Really, we all know that time is money
Why then do we wait for life to get sunny?
It's true; time doesn't wait for anyone
So isn't it time we all try to understand
Playing with time is such a big mistake
It kills our drive in what we undertake

Out of the rough
Never give up the fight,
For whatever is right.
Though living is tough,
We'll get out of the rough.

Doers
If you want to start a lifetime task,
Why stick with who only want to ask.
Never mind breathing weary doers,
Keep your focus on the can do areas.

Kept alive
Delay will make you nosedive,
But your dream must be kept alive
So-call friends will pretend to care,
Knowing this will prevent despair.
Stay close to the conscious light,
Then everything will be just bright.

The puzzle
When life isn't clear,
I've got to persevere.
Sticking with the puzzle,
All I have to do is hustle.

Fertile seed

In order to really succeed,
We'll have to plant a fertile seed.
Feeding our brain with the right attitude,
Idleness will never try to deceive or intrude.

Abundance
Lots of noise and no substance,
Only action can bring abundance.

New light
When nothing seems to be going right,
Tomorrow will bring a brand new light.

My view

Yes I'm talking to myself,
With ideas about my wealth
For years I have tried,
Yet success won't abide.
Time to change my view,
On the things I'll pursue.

Common sense

Let's not worship senseless vanity,
Then pretend we love humanity.
Why waste time with that pretence,
When all we need is common sense.

The lead

The more I try is the more I learn
Got to keep my focus and succeed
Whatever is lasting must be earned
Giving your all you'll take the lead

Smart work

Countless hours at your devotion
Nothing will ever get in the way
There will always be real solution
Smart work can show us the way

In sync

I can't afford to waste one minute
And watch my dream go to sleep
Have to spend precious time in it
Then my inspiration I'll truly keep
Today all the pieces have truly link
With the needed trimmings in sync

Quest on time
No one can keep you down,
When your plans are sound.
Don't wait for a special sign,
To start your quest on time.
Placing your goals in sight,
Finally, it will come to light.

Don't be discouraged

Dig a little deeper, being on the edge our
Dreams won't mature. Don't be discouraged
When all doors seem closed, cause hardship
Will crumble in the face of perseverance.

Will be yours

Yes times are tough; everything is in the rough,
But don't lose sight of the will to do. Dig a
Little deeper, even when times get harder. The
Prize will be yours if you maintain the
Meticulous tasks.

Turn up the torch

Many loafers will criticize,
Cause they are dozing with laziness. When
doors are made of steel, turn up the torch
Much higher and melt away the mountain of
Hesitation. Remember when success is close
At hand, frustration always have a devious plan.

Come about
Be real and shed your conceited habits, we
Can still make it if we really try. All the good
Stuff we talk about will come about, if you
Are willing to join the Endeavour.

Right direction
No one can create success alone,
Doesn't matter how hard
They try. Self-discipline will push us in the
Right direction, if we can spare the time to put
Into practice our desires.

No middle ground
No middle ground if we really want self-
Liberation. Let's not encourage our lazy
Habits that will only bring us more
Uncertainty.

Love our-self
Now what are we doing to
Demand respect from others? It is mighty fine
To be people of color; it's time to love our
Self despite the brain wash influence of
Dividers.

Providence
Clearly, we can find the strength
Today to pursue our providence tomorrow.

A true virtue
Patience is a true virtue, which must be cared
For, or soon you'll lose it forever.
If we do not get what we want right away,
True patience should be given a chance.

To our rescue
When we cannot face tomorrow, the
Substance of patience will come to our
Rescue. When the night is still and no one is
Around to comfort you, remember to have
Patience in whatever you do.

Reach deeper
When we're Confused and depression won't let go,
It's time to reach deeper within our most inner
Strength. As we are trying to find our self,
Give patience a chance, and for sure you'll be
Invited to the celebration.

Clay-like dolls

What time is it? It's time to know ourselves,
Or they will make us into clay-like dolls and
Put us on a permanent shelve.

Natural qualities

Without them
God blesses our farmers, without them, we
Would all die from starvation. Other Professions
are looked upon as heroes, and what
Our farmers receive are big fat zeros.

Our appreciation
It's time We show our appreciation to all the farmers
Of the universe, they are not asking for much,
Just to be acknowledged for their
Contributions before they return to the dust

Way home

Sitting at the river's edge, the little fishes
Swim on the opposite side. Many birds
Singing different tunes, which keep my heart
In tune. The sun is going down now, so it's
Best if I find my way home.

Joy everlasting

Another golden sunset beyond the hills, its
Beauty lingers way into the evening. Doesn't
Matter if you live in a shack or castle, this
Sunset brings to us joy everlasting.

Ray of light

Without
Prejudice or malice a scattered ray of light
Dose the scenery with a kind of wholesome
Love, that is just for the taking, if you are
Living on the corridor of a spiritual nature.

Alside

Want to go back to Ballard's Valley,
Where the view make our eyes dally.
No, this is not really a joke or folly,
A trip to Alside will make you jolly.

Mist and rain
It's Friday again, we're off to the North
Coast. Linstead City, the City of mist and
Rain. Constant showers, which brings flowers
In April and June.

Spur Tree Hill
Going up Spur Tree Hill,
With several tons, the Land Rover cries for
Mercy. Many miles along the way, the Rover
Never fails us, even on a windy rainy day.

Flat Bridge
It wouldn't be wise to rough up the turn at Flat
Bridge; we might capsize and never be seen
Again.

Bog-Walk
Traveling through Bog-Walk fog so
Thick, you can hardly see. Passing through the
Luscious green brings true clearness from
Within.

Such Beauty
Up ahead a reminder of Mother
Nature on both sides of the road. Linstead
City, it's so pretty, driving through transcend
Such beauty.

Vibrant
Can you hear that vibrant tune?
You could easily tell it's a loon.

My weariness

Tried to rise from my bed this morn', but my
Weariness kept me in until the sunlight
Disappeared. Now the birds went home to
Sleep, their sweet music I've missed five days
In a row.

Summer time

As the sun rises in the summer time, it
brought sweet gift of energy to all who's in
Sight.

Scented flowers

Roses of many colors, will beautify our
Surroundings with all the rejuvenating we
Need. Scented flowers, they bloom all day
Long, now the sun's off to a distant land, but
Tomorrow it will be back vibrant and strong.

True light
Angel of true light guides us to do what is
Right. When we falter, leave us not to be in
Doubt. Help us to keep our thoughts in
Perspective, because it's so easy to be
Intercepted.

Guide us
Angel of true light guides us to do what is
Right. With all this destructive noise, teach us
How to be poised. Where all races are
Concern, isn't it time we live in peace

Safe flight
Angel of true light guides us to do what is
Right. Please take away the fright that lingers
Through the darkest of night. If only we could
Get a hold of the light, then tomorrow we
Would be able to glide and have a safe flight.

Meaty fruit

Star apple such a stingy fruit, when ripen, it
Will not share its meaty fruit. There it will
Stay, till the cows come home; never will it
Fall to the ground, even on a very windy day.
If you have ever tasted this star of a fruit,
Purple or green, I'm sure you'll make a
Scrumptious scene.

Always relish
Breadfruit, dumpling, ackee and codfish,
We'll always relish, just want to go back
Home to Jamaica so we can get it fresh.

Try All Top Hill
Try -All St-Elizabeth the W.I where I was
Born, most of the nation has so much warmth.
Jamaica as a whole, the people are so
Humble, they will give you their last cup of
Love.

Giant fruits
Today the seasons are changing; our
Fruit trees had all been rearranged. Long ago
Trees would just sit there and does nothing;
Nowadays they are bearing giant fruits that
Dangled from massive stems.

The river bank
Sitting on the riverbank, waiting for the birds
To sing. Automobiles of many sound
Constantly interrupting.

Tried to focus
Tried to focus on the
Birds ahead, but a wise guy shouted and they
Flew away.

Cool breeze
The cool breeze felt so refreshing;
Anything else would have to retreat.

Beautiful sight
The trees and river, truly a beautiful sight, they
Correspond with our senses with a pleasant
Delight.

From the air
Using bamboos in Jacky-hill,
Chang lured the birds at will.
Catching them every year,
As they take a rest from the air.

Place to remember
Seeing these birds of September,
Is a beautiful sight to ponder?
Jacky-Hill a place to remember,
That's where the birds flew over.

A sea of birds
Making this trip every September.
In the cool month of September
A sea of birds in the big blue sky
It's hard to ignore, even if you try.

Warmth and grace
Motherland of the human race,
Your beauty is of such warmth and grace.
They tried to smash your beauty from within
Still your gracious love is the real thing.

Mother Africa
The follies of the world can't compare,
All the love that you possess and share.
Mother Africa we'll always embrace,
Acknowledging her gift to the human race.

The bread winner

Some of us are trying to be thinner,
Do remember you're the breadwinner.
Looking good is our universal right,
Then keep it safe in all types of light.

Listen

Listen to the rapid beat of your frightened
Heart, don't get carried away, cause it might
not restart.

Smiling faces

Long ago friends with bright smiling faces,
Brings joy to your soul, which wealth can't
Replace. The warmth flows deep within our
Heart that's why some friends will never go
Away. Their kindness reminds us of the good
Old days, days that we'll never let go.

Magical ride
While waiting on Flight 983, I met Scarlet.
Moments later we discussed the philosophies
Of Marcus Garvey. With Scarlet by my side,
Life will be a magical ride.

Sincerely

Inner peace shouldn't be a difficult task; it
Will participate if you sincerely ask. Life is a
Beautiful thing when it's shared; nothing in
The whole world can compare.

World-wide epidemic

Vanity
Today it's a world-wide epidemic
People's lives are ever so cheap
The need for vanity is never-ending
Young life snuff out without hesitation
And you'll pay for your involvement
Walking around without a bit of remorse

Suffers
Tomorrow you'll get up for your new day
While relatives of the young man suffers
Though you think you're mighty and strong
If you live to be old, guilt will suffocate your
Existence.

Quiet lunch
To really find a calm place,
Those days have been erase.
Can't even have a quiet lunch,
Useless noises come by the bunch.

Our brood
You can call him whatever you want, so they
Call him whatever they want. Never mind the
Respect, which should be given. Doing what
They want to do, our broods were auctioned
Off to the highest bidder.

When groom
 As we get older,
Time appear to move faster. Yes, I know most
Likely, they won't care for him. Especially,
When groomed at such a young age. Doubt if
He will ever see them again, but do you think
That will ever ease the hurt

To permeate
Bullies in our schools, break the rule,
At times they can get very, very cruel.
They brought fear to their schoolmate,
As they waited after school, to permeate.

If you are different
Bullies will take out their frustration,
On bystanders without provocation.
Love to hate you if you are different,
Then leave you without one red cent.

All over the nation
Teachers are in a difficult situation,
Worse of all it's all over the nation.
Some parents are trying to help out,
While others point fingers and shout.

Back of a hearse
Every year it's getting worse and worse
Victim's final ride is in the back of a hearse.

Catastrophe
Watch what you're doing, cause the
Passionate eye won't lie. They will root out
The mystery and shed light on the catastrophe.

Undone
The world at large can pretend, but the
Passionate eye, the truth it will defend. When
You've abused the rights of others, in due
Time your lustrous future will become
Undone.

Terrified rage

Jimmy went downtown and loses his crown
The cops kept on searching but it couldn't be
Found. Days later, an old lady was passing
By, there was Jimmy's head filled up with
Lead, hidden so innocently, with tears running
Down her face, she screams in a terrified
Rage, saying out loud why can't our young
People turn over a new and loving page.

Very cold

There I was worrying about the future at
Eight years old, and hardly started to live in
The present time. It's as if the whole world
Was on my shoulder, seeing how some people
Can become so very cold.

Permanent run
Don't show off your scared self with a gun,
Cause soon you'll be on a permanent run.

Whatever
Much time spent on hurting each other,
Finding whatever is required to smother.

Increase
Excuse, thank you, and please, is decease,
That's why much damage is on the increase

Trust

With honesty and trust,
Longevity is a must.

Useless

Waste not your time,
Committing useless crime.

Revoked

Sitting in prison is not a joke,
Cause your liberty will be revoked.

Deliberately

Why can't we have compassion, instead?
We're pumping lead in our brother's head.
Why are we deliberately trying to eradicate
The human race, then speaks of liberty for
Those who can hardly keep up the pace.

Ever do

How can tomorrow be bright?
When all we ever do is fight.

Unwanted rage

Whether morning, noon or night,
We will destroy what's in sight.
Time to take life to a higher stage,
And get rid of the unwanted rage.

Kindness & devotion

Love knows no color
Love knows no color,
Yet some hearts so hollow.
We may pretend for a while,
Then realize it's out of style.
Foolish hate may linger,
But true love's the master.

Why pretend
Save your tears, why pretend that you really
Love me. Soon I'll no longer have to worry,
Cause I'll be taking the southbound train.
You don't even have to remember my name.
I'm so tired of your foolish behavior, if I
Stick around, surely I'll go insane.

No need
No need to wipe the tears, because they're dry
Anyway. Stop pretending we're still in love,
Cause we no longer care.

Been replaced
Don't have to call me on the phone, our time has run its course.
We must go our separate ways, now that our
Love has been replaced.

Anymore
Won't try to hold on
Anymore, it's time to see what is real. I'm
Sure we'll remember a good moment here
And there, but the bad times won't be far
Away.

For a life time
A spiritual woman I've found, she just wants
To make me dance. Her mystical smile is one
Of a kind that I will treasure for a lifetime.
She speaks of honesty, now I will be a true
Optimist. Her charm awakes me late at night,
Then I'll have to kiss her precise.

Take my heart
Lips so tender and satisfying,
They tend to agree with
My motive. Mystical woman, take my heart,
So we'll never be at a distance. Today I've
Found someone whom I believed to be
Profound. Her charm awakes me late at night,
Then I'll have to kiss her precise.

A little bit closer
I'm here thinking life would be nicer,
If my lover were just a little bit closer.

Pretentious
Pretending that she really, really care
All I've got is a pretentious love affair

Lonesome
Weeks and years have gone on by,
But here I've remained a lonesome guy.

Got to dear to love
We've got to have love, before we can give
it. We've got to share love, before we can enjoy it.

No boundaries
We've got to dare to love, before
We can claim it. Love, true love, knows no boundaries.

A splash of forget me not

She tried to get my attention, but is it love or
Lust. Her beauty melts my most inner being;
And her perfume gives a splash of forget me
Not. Can't get carried away, because some
Would- be love never stayed.

Love or lust

I'll try not to
Show that I'm anxious; don't want to give her
The wrong impression. I've got to wait and see
If she's fi-real, is it love or lust.

So much energy

Who will pick you up when you're down?
It takes so much energy just to get around.
If there's no soul mate to raise you up again
Your confidence might endure a lot of strain.

Our life
Don't waste our love with foolish game,
Because our life would never be the same.

Keep at bay
Won't need approval if this or that say,
Those friends we've got to keep at bay.

Different
To be different, they think we're foolish,
But we won't sit down and live sluggish.

Move forward
We've got to move forward right now
Applying our energy where times allow.

Negative people
Can't have negative people around us
Whose ambition is to constantly fuss?

Living free
Living free of tangled debris is essential,
It will give us strength, which is crucial

Her beauty

Met a little jubbie from out a lane,
Suddenly my heart finds its aim.
Now I've really got to confess,
Her beauty put my nerve to the test.
I know I shouldn't get carried away,
But her smile leads my heart astray.
You might say that I was a bit weak,
But this little jubbie was very unique.

Our African Queens

Free up our Nubian princesses, don't you
Ever keep them in misery? Our African
Women we must learn to protect, why then
Are you exchanging diamond and pearls for
Our African Queens. Have you all lost your
Imprudent minds?

Hidden mask

Shed not your lonely tear, cause now we're
Apart, maybe what we both need is a fresh
Start. Trying to find the perfect girl is a
Labor of love, cause some people wear a
Hidden mask. Guess I'll keep on living
Without my angel of a bride, this tidal wave
I'll continue to ride.

Coldness and laziness

Infected seeds

Hatred and greed, always breeds a multitude
Of infected seeds. There you are, talking
About good deed, but your scrupulous deeds,
Always hurt someone in need.

Intrigued

You say I know where this is going to lead,
And then you bleed the will of the people and
Destroy their thirsty trees. These fools
Seemed intrigued by your coldness of
Brutality, because you had dissected their
Self-determination unfortunately.

Covered

So many eyes have been covered with
Laziness, and now the whole damn world is in
A major crisis.

Guide ourselves

How about "Us" instead of "I," How about
"We" instead of "My," How about ours
Instead of yours. We need to guide ourselves
Out of these chains of going nowhere
With selfishness.

Kind of urge

It's not about knowing this or that,
That kind of urge would have to be cleansed.
The contribution of love can cause no pain
We better start giving it now, or we all will
Go down the drain.

Corrupted humans
I'm here to expose the corrupted humans,
Who practice a two-tier system?

Overloaded fools
Thinking, they are better than other people, some
Overloaded fools are demanding to be treated as superiors

Elusive influence
Crippling society as a whole,
They buy their way to the front of the line.
With brains no bigger than a nut, they show
Off their elusive influence.

Spoils
And so, morality
Is vaguely mention, yet every chance they
Get, they share the spoils corruptively.

Hard to handle

Commercial living destroying our life,
And it's so hard to handle the strife.
Some say bigger is actually better,
But who's receiving all the glitter.

The needy

The needy being robbed as we speak,
As a better life they are trying to seek.
Downsizing comes in many cute names,
Yet we know who's pocketing the gains.
Bare face crooks are the name of the game;
They are design to drive the innocent insane

Rainy day
Another nightmare last night,
Nothing seems to be going right.
These outrageous bills out of control,
In the end, they might just take its toll.
Tried to put a bit away for rainy day,
But inflation eats most of it away.

Dwindling
Purchasing power dwindling as we speak,
We haven't gotten a raise and it looks bleak.
Greedy down pressers pretending they care,
Treating us unfairly with no change to spare.

Insomnia
When our eyes are covered with what we
Should have or what we've acquired, a life of
Insomnia we'll learn to regret.

Sometimes
Life isn't all
About wanting everything we see; sometimes
It's about giving generously.

World's ego
Much happiness
Has been wasted, thinking of the world's ego,
Only to realize the mistake they've made.

Long road
We are so nice, protecting the people who
Deceived us. Trying to buy friendship at any
Cost, and deliberately forgetting that they are
Traitors of life.

Convoluted
The future has us in the dark,
Now a long road we'll have to travel. The
Present times we think is good, but look
Around and you can see our existence is
Really convoluted.

The bait
So we have a good job,
Then our great fortitude they will steal. We
Are so nice, we've settled for second best
While the hungry downsizers run away with
The whole prize.

Slender string
We are hypnotized by the
Bait they put before us, not seeing the trap
They have created on a slender string.

To enhance
Speaking of the people and their suffering is
Not a popular subject. It exposes the culprits
Who use them in order to enhance their own
Way of lofty living.

Blistered heart
They will cover up the
Blistered heart of the common people and
Then pretend this is the way it should be.

Years of pain
As these years of pain become more
Unbearable, you must be tough to handle
These atrocities.

Perish
Economical enslavement of
The have not, has driven them under ground
And there they will eventually perish.

Fare share
Some of us give so much unwisely thinking that
Being some sort of a second hand banana the
Dominator will someday feel sorry and give
Us our fare share of the pie.

Appetite
Please don't wait
To be pity, cause their appetite has no ending
Sight and worse of all, they think that it's all
Right.

Withered
Don't cry when your money tree withered and
Die. All those years we've slaved for you and
All we've got were the crumbs from the table.
Greed has mastered your only way of life,
Now we can see your empire's tumbling
Down.

Courage
We've gotten into the cars this
Morning crank up the engine as it screams
Out before starting. Thirty below zero and
You've got to have the courage of a hero.

Long overdue
Only after we've reached the workplace, the
Heater started to function just a little bit. Then
We'll work with your ungrateful way of
Existence, only to pay some of our bills,
Which is long overdue with added interest
In pursue.

Reinstate
High tech cheaters only goal is to cheat the
Underprivileged. We have been cheated out
Of revenues and it's time for them to reinstate
What's ours. We may be nervous, but
Remember the takers won't give it back
Without a fight.

Our suffering
Sitting here writing these
Poems isn't hard, we only have to look
Around us and the evidence of our suffering is
Everywhere.

Can't escape
High tech greediness trying to
Destroy all signs of humanity, but never mind
Those cruel beasts, their inhumane nature they
Can't escape.

Distracted mind

Jealousy arise in a distracted mind,
And lasting peace you'll never find.
Don't desire the fruit of another,
It's time to find your own endeavor.

Clashes
Ungratefulness is your greatest passion
Scorning the commitment of the masses
Who treated you with true compassion?
More and more you're promises clashes

Selective
Cause greed is your only objective
Ignoring the hardship that is around
Giving perks to your very selective
Then expect us to treat you profound

No longer pretend
From now on, we'll no longer pretend
That you are really a caring person
Making sure your control is apprehend
Now that you're dictating have worsen

Your lies
We'll expose your lies from the start
And from society you'll slowly depart

Conceited

The harder we really work,
The more greediness smirk.
Hiding in suspicious places,
Bosses with conceited faces.
We are so weary and tired,
Soon we won't be for hired.

Downsizing

Downsizing is the name of the game,
Which leaves most workers in pain?
Workplace principles is now dead,
The working people can't get ahead.

Self-centeredness
Double standard is destroying the Holy Grail
Of humanity, which is certain to shorten life's
Expectancy.

Crying for peace
Today we're crying for peace,
Yet tomorrow we are as greedy as yesterday.

Disregarded
We've disregarded the cause of universal
Distress, with our hearts open to self-
Centeredness.

Lawmakers
Life could be better if they would stop
Digging into our purses. We don't have
Money to spend. But greedy lawmakers think
We are their takers.

Their feast
Seems we can't get away
From these heartless beasts. They have no
Conscience, and very proud of their feast.

Designed
Doesn't matter if your car is old or new, all
Governments are designed to ticket you.

Hidden taxes
The protest continues working harder, and
Being paid lesser. Can't keep up with the
Hidden taxes, it just make our foundation
Collapses.

Morality
Government playing tricks as more
Workers struggles, morality is lost in the
Ditch, and it must be found so it can be stitch.

Drips slowly

The reminder of death drips slowly from that
Big oak tree. They'd hang the whole family,
One cold and bloody night. Though they
Struggled for the right for liberty and life,
They still execute the helpless worn out souls.

For riches

The love for riches has be-clouded the human
Race, now a great promise of contribution
Is at a total lost. Today as the world pretends
Everything is running smooth, the blood is
Still dripping from that big oak tree.

Unbearable

It's July third, and the heat is unbearable in
The factory where we work. The temperature
Makes some worker's go off their rocker,
With no recourse to take. Ventilation is
Nowhere to be found, as the owners are too
Cheap, they expect us to work and don't make
A sound.

One by one
When you've got lots of money, everybody
Wants to be your best friend. As soon as the
Money is done, they'll leave one by one.

Yours and mine
Playing tricks is a national past time; most
People want what's really yours and mine.

Won't cry

Won't cry no more when they try to
Persecute the truth, cause truth has the power
That no one can demolish. When my days get
Longer and nights are colder won't cry any
More.

My luck

When I'm down on my luck, still I will
Cry no more. Life will always deliver, when
You've put in the work, the answers you seek
Is never far away when you refuse to give in.

Bit of sanity
They will snitch till their heart's content. In
The work place, grown human snitching away
The last bit of sanity they now have then
Tomorrow our children's, children will still be
In distress. Making the rich, richer.

At the expense
These full time snitchers someday hope and
Pray that they will be secured, but the only
Thing they will receive is a bucket of shaving
Cream. They are trying to live a life of
Significance, at the expense of others.

Betrayal
These snitchers shouting out for freedom, but
For them that day will never come. They will
Die within the walls of betrayal, which they
Have set up for their foolish protection.

Emptiness
Nothing can save the traitors of emptiness
That preyed upon the existence of honesty.

Fruitless

Everyday snitchers living a life of make-
Belief, trying to snitch their way to a big
Promotion. A sense of security occupied their
Fruitless selves, and sadly, they will introduce
It to the children of tomorrow.

Working class

Days had gone by, months has gone by, years
Has gone by, centuries are a thing of the past,
And for the working class the world stand
Still. Self-destructive snitchers are ever so
Blind, their eyes are covered by arrogance
And we'll now have to let them be.

Cubbyhole

I'm sure the key to our success won't be lead
By these snitchers, they have peep through
Any little cubbyhole they can find only to
Inform on the working people. Why is it so
Hard to understand that whenever we snitch,
We'll also feel the sharp edge of the push?

Decayed

While most of us pretending that life's okay,
Our way of living has steadily decayed.
Workplace atrocities mounting higher than
Everest, as hungry beast is in for the big kill.
Some workers treated like second hand tools
Then made to look like pointless fools.

Global quest

Promotions for the deprived will have to
Work twice as hard, and still they won't
Receive a fare wage. Isn't it time we cut out
The root of our downfall, then look at the
Cause of the problem? Waste not your time
Destroying another, that's not the solution to
Your global quest.

Blood of others

The only benefactors of
This obstruction are the suppressers and that's
A horrible way to live. They may try to enjoy
The blood of others, but soon time will catch
Up to them. We must cut each other's throats
Just to pay the rent, and yet they are not
Satisfied.

Seekers

A worker who has not the
Inclination of their strength from within,
Searching for liberty they just don't know
Where to begin. Freedom seekers just
Remember if you seek a little bit longer in a
Different place, you will find your true
Vocation.

To refresh
When one's brain is factorized, it's totally
Hypnotized and very difficult to refresh.
Devoting your livelihood to the factory, cuts
Off any chance of achievement, which in time
We'll learn to resent.

New insights
 A quick paycheck is
Enticing, but those trees won't bear the best
Fruit. To free up our brains, we must open our
Minds to new insights from within ourselves.
Only suggesting we should take the
Necessary chances to become what we really
Want to be.

It's time
It's time we are awake from this
Lifeless slumber. We will neglect our own
Dreams and build other people's reality. Now
You have received the sustenance to plant
You're thirsty seed, make the most of the time
You've got in every way that you can ever
Imagine.

Labeled

Hard working men and woman do exist, the
World does not comprise of suit people only.
Today society has ignored and labeled all the
Hard working people of the world. As these
Lines are written, strategies are being
implemented how to keep the unfortunates
Behind closed doors.

Pencil pushers

Today we only heard of
The pencil pushers as if they are the one
Who's providing the essential food, clothing
And shelter, isn't it time, we all recognize the
Genuine providers of the universe.

Negative

What is it with this negative "n" word? We
Have it for coffee, breakfast, lunch, dinner
And snacks then we demand respect from
Other nations. The airway is stifled with it,
Some of us embrace it, even making loads of
Money and pretending that it's the in ting.

Both ways

Remember what happen when we sit and try
To arise at the same time. Now we'll have to
Expose these hypocrites who want to have it
Both ways.

Self-respect

It's time to educate ourselves,
Before we are totally removed from the face
Of the earth. For years, self-respect has been
Under house arrest and hardly anyone really
Notice.

Will pass
When tears of sorrow surrounds you, fear not
Of your lonesome heart. The painful burden
Of the tragedy will pass, and then the sun will
Rise with its vital warmth.

Unexpected
We're all faced
With unexpected worrisome task, but real
Answers will draw closer and ease the hurt.

Personal quotes

Reach on time
Punctuality will get mix reviews, so much
Excuses and stores they'll make you blue.
Punctuality is good medicine when taken at
The right time, and then early you must go to
Bed so wherever you are going you'll reach
On time.

Good benefits
I've got a few friends who aren't so
Punctual, but with some persuasion they now
Agree that it's a good transformation. There
Are a lot of good benefits from being
Punctual, for one thing we don't have to rush
And then cause uncertain arrival.

I do believe
I do believe
Being punctual is the tool of survival; it gives
Strength to those who grasp it with good
Intention. Punctual people always stick
Together; any storm they can surely weather.

Excuses
Excuses for me I must refuse, because
Punctuality can serve as our own betterment.
All you late comers and doers wipe the slate
Clean then your life will be almost complete.
What you now deny, could be your passage
To true freedom?

Be loyal
Love is of splendor when trust is guarantee
When there is no surprises waiting for you
Giving completely, we will never disagree
That we should be loyal in whatever we do

Regardless
Regardless of the bait that they've presented
Years of friendship should never be dented
Today some of us looks contentedly engage
With laughter attach, as if they're on stage

Misgiving
Whatever that will endure must be genuine
Deceits have no place in harmonious living
As we try to put food on the table and shine
Not forsaking your defender with misgiving.

Elusive
We shouldn't chase after an elusive alliance
When we can see a red flag with its defiance

Birthdays

Birthdays are a beautiful celebration, it
Furnish a brighter situation. We'll have
Laughter and songs of passion, singing loudly
Without confusion. Sharing real gift of joy,
Life is a precious gem that sparkles even in
The dark.

A mother

A mother of love, by your children
You are dearly loved. Forthright you are with
Your ambition; you go right ahead without
Indecision. Happy birthday Debbie and have
Fun, remember we'll love you always.

True example

Novlyn, your kind heart reflects who a true
Being is. As a giver, you shall forever be of
Real love. You are a true example of what the
World need, planting the seed of love that we
So really need.

Caring ways

As we watch you since we
Were younger, you're caring ways make us
Much stronger. At times when we are weak
We look to you for guidance, cause you're so
Unique.

Greatest trait

You have taught us over the years,
How to be aware. To share is one of your
Greatest traits, and hate can never infiltrate.

Never far

A Caring mother you are, your children's love is
Never far. You are one of a kind, always
Putting others first with true love in mind.

Destination

Dedication is one of your favorite obsessions;
You have made many a sacrifice to reach
Safely at your destination.

Clear to see

 It's clear to see the
More birthdays that you celebrate; it shows
Your positive trait. Kindness from you is a
Plus; you'll even take the long way home if it
Meant to be just.

Happy birthday

Happy birthday Michelle
With lots of love from Ainsley, Ashley, Ethan
And us, a mother at heart with eternal loving
Trusts.

Looking pretty

Ashley is our latest princess; she sat there
Looking pretty, in her little pink dress. Her
Smile makes a dull day brighter and
Happiness from within can only thrive.
With two bottom tooth she looks quite astute.
Cuddling in her mother's arm, she looks at
Her dad, with a true sense of love and calm.

Family tree

Your kindness bloom over our family tree
Causes your love for all of us shines so
Excellently in times of need you comfort us?
Without making any sort of fuss?

Great mom

A great mom you are
 Who cares for your children and
Other children are of the world.

Giving

Giving is your life's work; anything less just
Wouldn't work. Your siblings do love you;
We say many thanks for all the things you do.

Abundant

Your children's love for you is in
Abundant, cause they know caring for them
You're never reluctant.

A natural trend
As we congregate for another birthday,
Togetherness is so heartily. Times moving
Expediently, seems we're having birthdays
More frequently.

Together
It's good to celebrate our
Birthday with family and friends, it keep us
Together with a natural trend. Those you've
Inspired, have acquired their desire. Happy
Birthday Jessie and have fun, remember we'll
Love you always.

Free

Wherever we'll be, have to remain brisk and
Free. Won't hesitate to infiltrate all negative
Destructive traits. Remembering where we
Have to go, keeping the true inner light a
glow.

Time

 As time moves on, seeing what life
Have to offer, never losing sight that
Tomorrow will have the answer. Facing the
Struggles together, learning how hard a life
We must weather.

Guiding hand

 Standing firm with
Enduring plans, we'll find our castle that will
Be so grand. The truth with the guiding hand,
Won't be far when we need a hand. Knowing
That dreams come true, we'll search for the
Tools to do

Everyday task
As friends we've gone separate ways, but
True respect will always stay. Though they
Have tried to dissect our friendship, our
Brotherly love can never face hardship. Going
Through life's everyday task, we'll have to
Keep the faith to face each and every task.

New beginnings
New beginnings will be different; we just
Have to learn how to make the adjustment.
Respect you have demanded from everyone,
That's why our friendship will always have the
Upper hand.

Calm sea
Friendship is the foundation, the foundation
Of any honest situation. Through the years
We've face many rough seas, but we
Reminded each other of the calm sea to be.

Life can
Facing the struggles of today and tomorrow,
Life can be overwhelming with our sorrows.
Remembering those who's worse off, we
Gladly appreciate what we now enjoy.

Persistency
Years
Have rolled beyond our wildest dream, yet
Mutual respect remains the only theme.
Before us will be new challenges, face them
With persistency.

Tranquility
 With tranquility on our
Side, we shall move with grace through life.
True friendship is forever; they guide us
Through all endeavors

Chief aim

The quest for liberty is your chief aim in life,
Though it's an uphill battle, you'll always
Strive. Remembering the reason for such a
Huge task, we'll be giving our support without
Been ask.

Willingness

 For all "who" puts in the effort for
The cause, we salute you with all our heart. It
Takes a willingness to give, and for you that's
The only way to live.

Enlighten

Interruption will show
Their disruptive faces, then they'll be
Enlighten and shown their rightful places.
Self-empowerment is your destination;
Together we'll find the solution.

Desire

As I am for you and you for me, let love rule
Our destiny. When troubled times try to
Obstruct our plans, we'll remember where our
True hearts belong. So glad we are, that we've
Found each other, now we can share our love,
As we desire.

Ponient love

Cause love is what we've truly
Found; anything less we'll surely frown.
Where trust is concerned, time has showed
It's earned. So remember now that we have
God's blessing, our ponient love will live
Forever.

Each other

Through thick and thin, sadness, joy
And happiness we'll be together. Reaching
Out for each other was the best thing to do, so
Let love rule .As you for me, me for you.

Kindness
An African rose you are, giving so much love
To the rest of the world. Treating everyone
With kindness, then you shall live free in
Trueness.

Share
As you love to share in your doing,
Then we shall wish you and your family good
Luck in all you're doing.

Respect
With respect from us
To you, we know that life's gonna treat you
Good in whatever you do.

Goodbye

So you didn't have the courage to say
Goodbye. Giving your friend the letter that
Put me in a daze. We use to have such a good
Time. A day doesn't go by, that I don't think
Of you. Treated me like a king, but didn't
Have a chance to treat you like a Queen.

Will always

Sitting here just wondering how different life
Could have been, if you had chosen to stay.
Whatever transpires in life, I will always
Remember you and I know you feel the same
Way too? Your tender loving care is never far
From my mind. Where are you now? Seems
My love for you will never expire.

Kind hearted

A wholesome lady we've known for a long
Time, a loving kind- hearted friend that gives
Her all, all the time. She treats who's around
Her with great respect, then her daily living it
Does reflect.

Cherished

Honesty is cherished as time
Goes by, could not hurt another even if she
Tries. Living a life of wholesomeness,
Bonding with Leo with blessedness. With
Truly blessedness

A rear gem
Compassion is like a rear gem these days,
Most people who give just want to be paid.
We've experience the nature of your giving
Ways, a combination of trust and care, you've
Share with the rest of the world.

Assurance
We are sure
This kind of inner strength will be passing on
To the next generations, with assurance that it
Will be of great celebration. Kindness can be
 The bridge for all beings, ''who'' need to
Cross to the other side of certainty.

True grace
To start a
Task we should, but to finish is the ultimate
Dream. You are always willingly reaching out
To make a difference, for that you shall
Receive such true grace from within.

What's right
Dereck is a true scholar, the fallies of life he'll never acquire.
Standing up for what is right, he won't give up, and he'll fight.
Many a men tried to persecute him, but their chance was very slim.

Many storms
So many years working together, we've weather many storms; these memories will last forever. We've traveled on that bumpy road for long time, but now, as we look back, it's all fine.

Forward
Facing the years to come, with clearness to see beyond. The road has been paved for a joyful life, now go forward cause you can only strive.

Way of life

For you, being determined is a way of life,
Knocking down all kind of strife. You know
What it takes to reach your goals, never
Embracing lazy strolls. Watching you from a
Distance, you are all persistence.

True hearted

As we
Defend truth and rights together, those days
Will always be remembered. There is a
Different way of life for truehearted friends,
Because the truth they always defend.

Inline
Slow and steady, soon your destiny will
Come. Travelling too fast could be out of
Control. The time has come to be conscious,
Conscious of which road is clear. Life
Experience is the teacher of time, so get back
In line with your journey in mind.

A doing heart
When we
Have the will to become, the world will
Accept our decision. Don't be afraid to take
Charge of any situation, even though you are
Surrounded by frustration. Think of winning
No matter how small, cause a doing heart can
Never fall.

The ships
The ships you've sent out forever
So long will know that home is where they
Belong. Staying close to nature its
Blessedness, a life of trueness, brings forth
Sureness.

Won't be bleak

True inspiration is from our inner most, and
Then we'll let it loose where it's needed most.
Sharing wisdom with the weak, so their
Tomorrow won't be bleak. To give is a
Liberating force, it guides hungry souls then
They'll take the right course.

From the heart

An honest life is
The best; there's no competition to see who is
The best. Ras Shiloh an emissary at heart, a
True inspirator that teaches from the heart.
With uplifting messages that won't leave
Ever, you've given us the tools of awareness
That will be with us forever.

Repatriate
We are the opals of each other's heart, then
How could land and sea keep us apart. As we
Wait to repatriate, we only have to keep the
Faith. We'll remain in unison of true love,
Cause we were meant to be like a pair of
Inseparable doves.

Together
Struggles of our future
Will try to interfere; we only have to remind
Each other how much we really cared. As our
Children are the love of life, together we can
Only strive. Gia, you're sweeter than all the
Jasmine flowers of the world, Christopher,
Your tender love is as fresh as the mountain
Zest, that only true love can impress.

Cross over
Open- mindedness is a sturdy bridge; it helps
Us to cross over all kind of disadvantage.
Giving strangers the benefit of a doubt, it
Creates a climate of harmony that doesn't
Shout.

Tolerance
When we rush to past judgment, there
Can be no broad scope of betterment. The
World would be free of unkindness, if we
Could act with more tolerance and kindness.

Useless hate
With all the different tribes in the world, if
We could taste unconditional love for each
Other, this useless hate we wouldn't have to
Live under and suffer. When we can feel the
Pain that's been inflicted on the innocent, a
More beautiful world will be in existence.

Around us

As we can see, the love of humanity is in
You, because it reflects the things you say and
Do. At times it's hard to find people who
Care, but it's easy to detect that you really
Care. Around us are those who deceive to
achieve, we'll feel sorry for them and let
Them be.

Some days

 In time we will go our separate
Ways, but remembering kindness we always
Obeyed. Some days will be tough, thinking
About how life should have been, but we must
Dig much deeper, if we want to be seen.
There is a beautiful rose on a distant hill, go
Now and enjoy its fragrance until you have
Your fill.

My genuine rose

Prim is my genuine rose; to her I can't wait
To propose. Her tender heart has now bound
Us forever, and it's time to spend the rest of
Our years together.

Guiding light

Primrose, take my heart
Lover of all loveliness, without your guiding
Light my boat would surely run a wreck.

Bright taste

Woman of such bright taste, reaching home
I've got to make haste. With a blend of love
And kindness, I'll await your receptiveness. I
Can rely on your inner beauty; because
Honesty is your only duty.

Prime

Prim I'm gonna
Fill your cup with true love, all the way up to
The brim.

Gentle prose

My sweet rose, with such gentle
Prose. Understanding the rough cuts of life
You are here for me, then I'll never dish you
Hearth no matter how frustrating life might
Be. Primrose stay close to my heart, cause in
Life or death we shall never part.

Endless time

Ups and downs
The passing of time brought us more in line,
With what is really important today. In
reality we lived in a world of ups and downs,
busily trying to figure out what to complete.

Beyond
Excitement of the world trend stretches way
beyond and when death is at hand, everything
seems so insignificant. Not saying for you to
search for tribulation, but these are
uncertainties we all have to face.

Petite existence
 Have you
ever thought of getting old and helpless, it
brings a chill to our mind's eye? We'll miss
those who went before us, and then time will
destroy our petite existence.

Late before
The School bell rings, but she wasn't sitting at her desk. Never had she been late before, and then slowly Miss Neil told us, she was no more.

Brown grip
Angela Brown was the kind of classmate, which never frowned. We'll always remember her with her little brown grip. And losing her we'll never come to grip.

Calmness
Calmness was her finest trait and that no one can ever debate. She will always be in our memories; we know she had a short journey to heaven. Rest our little angel; rest in the arms of the creator.

Three sisters
Rosa, Lynette and Shem, they were a natural blend. Three sisters that shared one common bond of love, a connection with kindness that only goodness can reflect.

Gaze quietly
Across from the
gully where they lived, all three homes in view of each other, they only had to gaze quietly and where help is needed it will be rendered immediately.

Gentleness
 They were true
examples of how siblings should live; their main goal in life was to give. A lifetime of lesson was given, for those who seek it. Their way of life was of gentleness, leaving in their path all pure blessedness.

Prosper
Their contribution
will be with us forever, showing us the way to prosper. A triple season of compassion was anchored in our mind and heart, then their true living will always give us a new start,

Way of life
 Honesty was the only way of life, and they have leaved us with a first class way to strive.

Our love

Our tears continue to flow, when it will stop?
No one really knows .Our love for Sandra
will never end; she was a true mother, sister,
niece, cousin and friend.

Good- bye

 Every time she
comes to mind, we'll keep her kindness in
mind. The time has come to say good- bye,
but her memories we will never let go. We
have grown together as one, so how can true
love ever disband.

God of mercy

 Oh true god of mercy;
release us from this painful flight. As our
heart ache from day to day, our love for her
will never go astray.

Our Sally forever

 She was a caring mom,
who provides for her children the best way
she could. Now she's gone out of sight, but
will never be out of our heart and mind. Ever
much so loved. Our Sally forever.

Time will
Though you have gone before us, we will never forget your gentle kindness. Time will not erode your memory from our hearts, even though you have departed.

Cherish
 We'll cherish the short time you have spent with us; your caring ways was tremendous. We had shed many tears of sadness, knowing that you are no longer with us.

Flower of love
As we put revenge out of our midst, then we'll plant a flower of love within. Feeling sorry for the culprits that brought about our lost, one day they will realized the significant of our lost.

Restraint
 Love is the master of our pain; it heals the hurt and brings forth restraint.

Flying high

Ivy Gordon, our true Gordon of love. We have no doubt that she's flying high with her two extra sets of wings, way beyond the Milky Way.

Free hate

Her kindness from within, have given us a bridge to cross in our times of troubles. We'll keep her Gordon of love free of hate and malice; because that's the only way we'll enjoy her Gordon of love.

Encouragement

Whenever we stumbled, a word of encouragement is never far away, she always take the time to put us on the right track. With four wings, good tidings she'll forever bring.

For ever love

Our true Gordon of love, flying high like a wholesome dove. Like a wholesome dove, whom we'll forever loved.

As we linger
Twenty years of struggles together, we work under many a pressures. As we linger in each other's mind, good memories we'll truly find.

With maturity
When friends are in one location, yesterday is always the conversation. Things we use to frown about, with maturity, no longer come about, doesn't matter where we go; our brotherly love will also glow.

Calm and quietly

We've made a promise to Cliff, to spread the word of love and honesty. Calm and quiet he was, never making useless fuss. Emphasizing the need for peace among mankind, he dwells on the foundation of pure love.

Forgiveness

It was a
pleasure to have work with him; he has opened our eyes to many uplifting things. As the sun sparkles on his words of forgiveness, we are sure he is resting in a bright light of peace. Always finding time to give, and so the goodness in him will forever lived.

He teaches

A teacher of kindness, he teaches by example. Now you're resting quietly beyond our reach, we'll remember that love is within our reach.

Dearest love
Judy and her dearest love, they were like the most beautiful doves. With true giving hearts, it's so easy for them to get a fresh start in whatever they had perused. Judy was our life and protector at all cost, never mind what's the cost.

Giving agenda
A woman of a giving agenda, she would take care of whoever was in need. With a multitude of things to accomplish, they would carry out each task until it was accomplished.

At peace
A true businesswoman, she was articulate in a life of adventure. As they rest quietly under the fruit trees, our heart is contented knowing they are at peace.

Our teacher
Our teacher is now resting quietly in his own space; let's learn from him how to love the human race. We'll miss Baton when we think of love; he is a true example of what the world is missing.

So clearly
We've cried tears of
sadness day and night; our love for him will forever shine bright. Many more tears will flow, because his kindness we'll never let go. His goodness, he shared with me, that's why I see so clearly.

Trueness
He speaks yesterday with a
loud voice strong with passion; today we'll remember his trueness without confusion. Our love will be with Eula and the children always, even though some of us are so far away.

A fisherman
Pedro's Florida Gal, the most reliable fishing boat of its time. It must have been tough handling the sails and ores; a fisherman job wasn't an easy chore. Walking down the steep hill of look out, it echoes when you slightly shout.

Abundantly
Don't lose your footing, cause
there will be a lot of looting. Florida Gal has been providing for the family for many years, catching fish abundantly.

Parted waves
 One dark and
cloudy night the storm came and Florida Gal parted waves into pieces, many tears had been shed granddad said, now that Florida Gal is dead.